FIX
YOUR
THOUGHTS

KEANDREA KELLY

ISBN 978-0-578-92543-1 (Paperback)
ISBN 978-0-578-92544-8 (Hardcover)

Printed in the United States of America

Thank you, Lord, for always loving, protecting, and guiding me.

To My Mom, thank you for everything you've sacrificed for me and given to me. I love you more than you will ever know.

To My Dad, I love you so much. Thank you for everything you've taught me.

To My Brothers, Charles & Martin, thank you for your support. I love you both and my nieces & nephews.

To Fabian, thank you for the endless love, support, and friendship. You are everything good in the world. Never doubt it.

To Amaka, Boo Wing, Carmen, Ciera & Ashley, Dana, Dominique, Eddie, Guyla,

Jamekia, Jaz, Kacy, LaReesa, LeRoy, Mama Gale, Mary, Racheal + Rachel, Shamika,

Shanita, Troye & anyone else I may be forgetting who encouraged me to follow my dream and write. I love you all.

In remembrance of Inetta & John L. Edwards, Clifford Carmichael, Bill & Lizzie Kelly,

Quindolyn Wingfield, and **Markeda Mims.**

Table of Contents

Introduction

We are what we think about. Our thoughts can either comfort and strengthen us, or they can defeat us. Research suggests humans can have thousands of thoughts per day. *Thousands.* For negative thinkers, this means reinforcing negative concepts every seven seconds.

Imagine having a friend who delivers negative news every seven seconds. Every seven seconds this friend rings you up to say, "You won't get that job." "You'll never find love." "You look hideous in that outfit." Or "That idea is dumb." Many of us would simply not tolerate it.

So why is it that we allow negative repeated thoughts from ourselves? Are you aware that you can change those thoughts? If you weren't before, I am delighted to tell you that *you can change your thoughts*. You can stop thinking negatively and change your life. No matter what you've been told or what you've been telling yourself, you can be happy.

For years, I struggled with negative thinking: guilt, fear, depression, heartbreak, family trauma – you name it. I visited counselors, therapists, psychiatrists, and took prescription medications. I fasted, prayed, and analyzed every aspect of my life. After searching high and low, I received this message: *fix your thoughts*.

Nothing about my life changed until my thoughts did. When I released my old way of thinking and being, I experienced a shift. Life flowed easier, and I became less rigid. I stopped contemplating ending my life and got excited about the prospect of living.

If you've struggled with those same thoughts, please know that it can get better. You, too, can get excited about the prospect of living. You can stop replaying negative events from the past, and you can release anxiety about the future. You can fix your thoughts. You only need to take the first step.

How This Book Will Help You

The chapters of this book are filled with exercises, affirmations, and prayers you can incorporate into your daily routine for lasting results. *Fix Your Thoughts* isn't just about your thoughts. It's about finding yourself, being yourself, accepting yourself, and loving yourself. It's a tool you can use on your journey to healing and for the rest of your life.

Chapter 1: Faith

For many of us, spiritual beliefs shape our view of the world. It's the lens through which we see ourselves and others. Our faith can anchor us in times of difficulty or weigh us down with feelings of guilt and shame. If our Higher Power is accepting, loving, and kind, we are more likely to see ourselves in the same way. But if the God we serve is filled with judgment, condemnation, and criticism, we run the risk of becoming that way also.

No matter what our religious beliefs are, the essence of faith is love. The core of spirituality is to see ourselves and others lovingly. Our faith may teach us to strive toward high moral standards and live righteously, but *it is important to love ourselves even when we fall short.* Remembering that God is love helped fix my thoughts on faith.

Throughout my childhood, I was taught a version of Christianity that didn't leave much room for the believer. I was to obey God at all times, serve God at all times, never question God, never defy God, and certainly, never anger God. These teachings helped create a great sense of fear toward God in my life and an even greater sense of uncertainty surrounding religion.

As I grew older, these feelings of fear and uncertainty disturbed me and caused me to struggle with my religious beliefs. I couldn't reconcile what I had been taught about God with the feeling I got in His presence. The God I felt in my spirit was open to questioning. He invited my emotions including doubt and anger. I wondered how this could be.

While battling thoughts of disbelief, I was invited to do a 30-day prayer challenge with required Bible readings. I began the challenge hoping to feel reassured and resolved in my faith, but just the opposite happened. Some of the passages caused me to question not only God but also the characters in the Bible.

In an attempt to uncover the truth about Christianity, I researched religion day and night. I was looking for definitive answers or evidence that could not be refuted. What I discovered during the process of searching was much more valuable. I found that I wasn't alone. People before me had experienced the same feelings of uncertainty regarding religious beliefs. They have also managed to work through them.

When I eliminated the fear embedded in me since childhood that kept me from questioning God, I was able to admit that I wasn't sure what to believe. I took inventory of those feelings piece by piece. I dug deep and asked myself the hard questions that I had been either afraid to ask or avoiding for so long.

Did I believe in God? What about Jesus? Were they the same person? What about Muhammed? Or Elijah Muhammed? And the Universe? Were there any spiritual beings who spoke to me? If so, which one(s)?

Evaluating my faith was one of the first steps toward fixing my thoughts. A large part of how I saw myself was based on how God saw me. If He condemned me, I condemned myself. If He didn't approve, how could I? My thoughts could not become positive until I rejected the unhealthy fear of God and received His love. Challenging what I was told for years led me to the right beliefs for myself. I no longer fear punishment from God for my mistakes. I am proud to serve a God who is loving, kind, and forgiving.

Whether your faith is rock solid or on shaky ground, remember that God is love. And love is the common ground of all creeds. If voices are telling you that you do not deserve the love of God, reject them. You do not have to be perfect to receive God's love. Your very existence is enough. No matter what you have been told in the past, you can receive God's love today. You only need to take the first step.

Repeat the following affirmation to yourself at the start of every day and throughout. It will help to remind you of what faith is about.

Affirmation 1:

God is Love. God Loves Me.

God is Love. God Loves Me.

God is Love. God Loves Me.

God is Love. God Loves Me.

God is Love. God Loves Me.

Chapter 2: You

Your life has meaning. God formed you with purpose and placed you on this planet to pursue that purpose. As a baby, you were innocent and perfect, knowing nothing, the most honest portrayal of the creator. And though the days of infancy may be far behind you, please know that you can always return to this basic truth. You have a purpose.

You were not created to live in a constant state of misery and unrest. If you struggle with feelings of depression and thoughts of self-hatred, visualize yourself as the creator does – honestly, innocently, and lovingly. *Who are you?* You are more than the criticism of others. You're also more than your accomplishments and titles. You're the divine design of the ultimate architect – God.

You are neither disapproval nor accolades. You are not the "bad child." You aren't the "most valuable employee." And you certainly are not the "ugly friend." You are the physical manifestation of God's love. You are 30 trillion cells of greatness – neither above nor below anyone else.

Embracing these principles can help you fix your thoughts on yourself. Solid self-knowledge leaves you less vulnerable to the judgment of others and shields you from enslavement by your ego. A healthy view of yourself can empower you to live freely, in pursuit of your spirit's purpose.

What are your thoughts on yourself? If you're anything like me, negative thinking may have permeated every area of your thinking, including your thoughts on you. For many years, I held onto damaging personal beliefs, some of which looked like this:

"I am unworthy."
"I'm a screw-up."
"I'm dumb."
"I'm fat."
"I'm inferior."
"Nobody wants me."
"I am not good enough."

This soundtrack played in my mind repeatedly. And because of those beliefs, I sought external validation by engaging in activities like people-pleasing, tolerating abuse, and self-deprecating. I over-gave, over-did, and over-shared for fear that if I didn't, I would be rejected. It wasn't until I addressed those beliefs that I was ready to eliminate those damaging patterns.

Where did the idea that I wasn't enough come from? And why was it so much easier to believe than the fact that I was? Therapy and reflection helped me identify how that belief developed and why the thought arose in my mind repeatedly. It was a cycle of negative reinforcement – a negative belief had been planted in me, and that belief produced negative behaviors. The consequences of those behaviors confirmed the original negative thought that I wasn't enough. The cycle had to be broken and following the three steps below helped me to do so:

Step 1: Recognize the belief.

Step 2: Reveal damaging behaviors that are caused by belief.

Step 3: Replace the belief (and the resulting behavior) with a positive one.

Consider the beliefs you hold about yourself. Are they positive? What about your beliefs on others? Is it possible you have been holding on to viewpoints that are pessimistic, critical, or untrue? If so, please take the opportunity to flesh them out. Identify these harmful opinions and follow the three steps above to help break the cycle of your negative beliefs.

Exercise 1: Replacing Negative Beliefs

Negative Belief:

_____

_____

Damaging Behavior:

_____

_____

New Positive Belief & Behavior:

_____

_____

Negative Belief:

_____

_____

Damaging Behavior:

_____

_____

New Positive Belief & Behavior:

_____

_____

Negative Belief:

_____

_____

Damaging Behavior:

_____

_____

New Positive Belief & Behavior:

_____

_____

Negative Belief:

_____

_____

Damaging Behavior:

_____

_____

New Positive Belief & Behavior:

_____

_____

Negative Belief:

_____

_____

Damaging Behavior:

_____

_____

New Positive Belief & Behavior:

_____

_____

Negative Belief:

_____

_____

Damaging Behavior:

_____

_____

New Positive Belief & Behavior:

_____

_____

Negative Belief:

_____

_____

Damaging Behavior:

_____

_____

New Positive Belief & Behavior:

_____

_____

Negative Belief:

_____

_____

Damaging Behavior:

_____

_____

New Positive Belief & Behavior:

_____

_____

Negative Belief:

_____

_____

Damaging Behavior:

_____

_____

New Positive Belief & Behavior:

_____

_____

Exercise 2: Creating a New Soundtrack

Use your new beliefs to answer the question, "*Who am I?*" Create a statement of identity that represents the person you're striving to become.

Here is an example: I am a kind, peaceful, & loving child of God encouraging others to see themselves lovingly. Create yours below. Repeat it as often as necessary for it to become your new personal mantra.

_____

_____

_____

_____

_____

_____

_____

_____

_____

_____

_____

_____

Chapter 3: Relationships

For better or worse, our relationships have influenced who we are today. Before we could feed ourselves, our relationships with family provided us food. Before we could speak, our relationships with teachers taught us to form words. Before we could reason, our logic was instilled in us by those closest to us, and a huge part of our thought process is a result of our relationships.

If we were trained to think negatively, we did –through no fault of our own. On the other hand, if we were nurtured with loving-kindness, we are more likely to operate from that familiar space. Many of our habits result from our upbringing, and if those habits are damaging, they have the potential to affect not only us but also those with whom we share a relationship. Where this is the case, we can replace those harmful patterns with new, positive, and productive ones.

In evaluating our relationships, we must recognize the behaviors that have served us well and distinguish them from those that have not. What practices have we adopted that, if passed along, could be beneficial? What have we learned from relationships that are worth teaching to someone else?

If you find that negative thinking and resulting behaviors have crippled your relationships, including the one you have with yourself, you can change. Fear, anxiety, poverty thinking, low self-esteem, criticism, and judgment have no place in your new thought process. Release those strongholds and step into the life you were created to live.

Family Ties

It's been proven that our childhood affects us in countless ways. Studies suggest that the amount of support and encouragement we received during the first years of life can have effects up to 30 years later. Some experts even believe childhood experiences can impact how our brains develop, leaving us with lifelong consequences. Humans need food, safety, love, approval, connectedness, knowledge, and faith. If any of these needs aren't met in childhood, negative feelings can arise and be detrimental for years to come.

As adults, we owe it to ourselves to address negative events from our past and work through the damage those events may have caused. The thoughts we have about our past affect our thoughts today. Our family dynamic may not have been perfect, but we can move beyond those trials and choose peace for our lives today. If you've survived traumatic experiences from childhood but are stuck with negative thoughts about that time, try the next exercise.

Write a letter to your younger self. Go back as far as necessary, be sure to give yourself room to express your thoughts freely and completely. Acknowledge your feelings, fears, and insecurities. Allow yourself to sit with the emotions that arise. Finally, shower yourself with all the love you didn't receive as a child. Make a vow to re-parent yourself, meet your needs, and heal your wounds.

Exercise 3: Dear (Younger) Me,

_____

_____

_____

_____

_____

_____

_____

_____

_____

_____

_____

_____

_____

_____

_____

_____

_____

_____

_____

_____

Friendships

Friendships can be a source of love, stability, and
comfort. Our friends are often some of the closest
people to us and the first ones with whom we share
ideas. This can be enriching if we choose to surround

ourselves with positive friends. However, if the people closest to us are toxic, negative naysayers that energy can transfer into our mindsets.

You've likely heard the concept that you are the average of the five people closest to you. Or even simpler, "Birds of a feather flock together." These theories, though debatable, possess some element of truth. People you spend time with will influence you. It's up to you to decide to spend time with people who will do so in a positive way.

Think about the people closest to you. How do they make you feel? Do they contribute to your health and happiness? Or is their contribution to your life overwhelmingly negative? Sometimes, isolation from certain people and their energy is required for us to grow. If there are friends in your life who encourage you to remain complacent, commit acts that aren't in keeping with your standards or values, or evoke feelings of negativity when you interact with them, do not be afraid to let them go.

Their actions may not be personal; they may be encountering trials of their own. They could legitimately not mean harm; it could be that they don't know any better. It's also quite possible that they find comfort in keeping both you and them in your current state of being – this is not your issue. Your task is to recognize who is positively influencing you and release those who are not.

How can you embark upon a journey to change your life when you are frequently surrounded by people who discourage that change? Your chances of success decrease with every encounter. When you begin your self-work, you may notice a shift in your friendships. Some may be inspired by you and want to join – allow them. Some may resist your change in fear of the unfamiliar – allow them. You are working on you FOR you. A positive relationship with yourself will attract healthy friendships.

Romantic Relationships

Our love interests can bring out a side of us that nobody else has ever seen, as our romantic partners tend to get the most intimate version of us. We share our secrets, discuss our pasts, make plans for the future, and even allow them to inhabit our bodies – talk about an energy transferal. Healthy romantic relationships can enhance our lives drastically, but toxic romances pose a threat much greater than we care to imagine.

Healthy love builds trust, vulnerability, and respect. We feel secure and at peace with our partners. We're able to operate as individuals and as part of a team. Both parties are comfortable in the presence and absence of one another. This type of romance can pour into our spirit and renew our Faith.

But when we love others or mislabel our strong emotions as love without first loving ourselves, feelings of jealousy, possession, and anger can arise. We find ourselves tearing down those we claim to love or allowing ourselves to be destroyed. This type of romance breeds insecurity and mental instability.

The key to entering a healthy romantic relationship is to first establish a healthy relationship with ourselves. Meaning, to properly love anyone else, we must first properly love ourselves. Another person cannot love us enough to fill the void that a lack of self-love creates. That is the work we must do for ourselves.

Taking the time to know ourselves, be ourselves, love ourselves, and accept ourselves can only make the love we share with another person greater. When we are healed and whole before entering a romantic relationship, it helps our partnership flourish. When we begin a romance looking to add to – not take away from – another person, the love we experience is multiplied.

It's important to evaluate our relationship even after it has begun. Are we engaging in toxic behavior and misrepresenting this as love? Are we possessive or being possessed? Are we abusive or being abused? Are we adding to the relationship, and is the same true for our partner? Taking inventory and being accountable can guide us in deciding whether to continue in the relationship or walk away.

The most important earthly relationship we will ever have is with ourselves. Anything harmful to us is not love. We cannot be more afraid to be alone than we are to walk away from what we know is not love. Our spirit recognizes love. It is warm in its presence. It is fulfilled. It is alive. Our spirit is also sensitive to what is ego posing as love, no matter how much we repress the gut feeling that tries to guide us away.

The way we love ourselves sets the standard for others to follow. When we demonstrate respect for ourselves, our lovers will respect us. When we communicate lovingly with others, we will receive loving communication. The energy and love we expend reverberate back to us. A healthy love for yourself will attract a healthy romance too.

Chapter 4: Health

Good health is more valuable than any material possession. Some would even say it's priceless, and yet, many of us take it for granted. The ability to breathe, speak, walk, and reason are blessings that – if you're anything like me – we don't necessarily think about until they are in jeopardy. Our bodies have endured so much and carried us through even more, and for that alone, they deserve some thanks.

Health is multi-dimensional – physical, mental, and social elements each represent a portion of our overall health. You may have encountered difficulty with aspects of your health. They may have even significantly impacted your quality of life, *but this does not have to be your story*. Your health, although vital, does not define you. In the presence and the absence of good health, you are valuable.

If you're taking this moment to reflect on your health, what are your thoughts? Are they positive? Do you feel appreciative of your current health status and optimistic about the future? Or is there a feeling of anxiety and unease surrounding your thoughts on health? If your emotions are more aligned with the latter, please be encouraged.

To the best of your ability, remain positive in your spirit. This positivity will undoubtedly assist you on your journey to good health. Our bodies are fields of energy comprised of cells. We can absorb both positive and negative energies and each has its effects on our health.

Time and time again, studies have shown that positive thinkers have improved health outcomes. From decreasing your chances of a heart attack to increasing your life span, positivity – and more specifically, positive thinking – has been linked to endless health benefits. What's more, the power to change our thoughts is available to each of us free of charge and can be reversed whenever we choose (though I would not recommend this).

But with matters as serious as our health, is it *that* simple? Yes, it's that simple. Poor health can carry profound consequences, but adopting positive thinking is the same process for all matters. Recognize negative thoughts. Replace them. Repeat.

You may choose to begin an improved narrative surrounding your health. You may wish not to lead conversations with people about how poor your health has been or to refrain from victimizing yourself at the hands of your health status. Maybe you can begin to speak positivity over your health – even before you can see it. Whatever route you choose to take, understand that any small step toward choosing positive thinking is a big win for your health.

Another way we can begin to view our health more positively is to show gratitude for health as it is. Each day we wake up is a blessing and we have the opportunity to give thanks for that blessing. If you'd like to begin transitioning from negative thinking about your health to positive thinking, the next exercise may be for you. Recite this prayer to demonstrate gratitude for your body and your health.

Prayer #1.

Heavenly Father,

Thank You for the gift of life. Thank You for blessing me with the ability to breathe, speak, walk, and reason.

Thank You for bestowing the blessing of health upon me. Create in me the desire to appreciate Your many blessings, especially my health. Please help me to not take my health for granted. Show me the way to think positive thoughts about my health. Keep me safeguarded from any negative thinking that may carry severe health consequences. Grant me the willpower and know-how to improve my health and relieve me of health burdens that seem impossible to bear.

Amen.

Chapter 5: Money

Health may be taken for granted, but money rarely is! In the minds of many, money reigns supreme. For such a small object, money is a BIG deal. And though money itself is useless (the physical paper and coins that is), the exchange of money for services and goods we obtain is more valuable to some than life itself.

I'm not a money expert, and I won't claim to be. But I've made six figures and zero figures, and there are lessons to be learned with both. If you've reached a considerable age, it's likely your thoughts on money are fixed. And it's even more likely that you have the evidence to support your thinking. But if you're open to it, I'd like to share some ideas with you that may help expand your financial point of view.

#1) Money Is Not the Root of All Evil

Gasp! Yes, I believe the apostle, Paul, said "...*the love* of money is the root of all evil..." So, if you've been living a life of self-imposed poverty to somehow align yourself with spiritual righteousness, I'm not exactly sure that's the way.

The love is a critical portion of that statement that is often eliminated from the recollection of this verse. Money itself is unproblematic. Money has perfected the art of minding its business until, that is, someone decides to go ballistic over acquiring it or not acquiring it. This is typically when evil reveals itself.

So, money has taken a bad rap for things it hasn't even done. And if you're one of those people who have thought for years and years that money is evil, it shouldn't come as a surprise if you have an unhealthy relationship with it. Do you have a healthy relationship with anything else you consider evil? The devil, for instance, or mass murderers? NO! Your thoughts on money work just the same.

The good news is, you can fix your thoughts on money. Money is a tool – nothing less and nothing more. Money is a resource that can help you improve your quality of life. It is not to be feared or condemned. And it is certainly not to be loved. Money is an inanimate object. And as with all inanimate objects, you can love it as much as you want, but the love cannot ever be returned.

#2) It's Not All About the Money

Contrary to popular belief and culture, everything isn't about money. Everything isn't always about any one particular topic, and money isn't the exception. While money is extremely important to certain people, it cannot be all things. At the risk of sounding cliché, let me expound. Money cannot keep you warm. Money cannot bring you a glass of water. And money cannot buy love.

Life is an array of experiences, emotions, and undertakings. Money may play a role in our lives, but our lives are not all about money. Remember the human needs we discussed in Chapter 3? They didn't include money, and for good reason – it's not a human need.

The emphasis placed on money is often misguided. Our needs for food, safety, and knowledge are often mistaken for a need for money. Because we associate our needs with survival and perceive money as a need, the thought that money is survival arises. Faced with the threat of survival, people have done things that they would not otherwise do.

If you've experienced similar thoughts before, it's never too late to re-train your brain. It's not all about the money. It is, however, all about safety, love, approval, connectedness, knowledge, and faith.

#3) More Money Does Not Mean More Problems

I, too, love this song. But like so many other fan favorites, it's someone's truth and not necessarily *the* truth. More money does not have to mean more problems. Different problems? Probably. More problems? Not necessarily.

Negative thinking about money impacts our relationship with money. Do you want more problems? Probably not. If you've internalized "more money, more problems" as truth, it is likely that the opportunity for more money has been extended to and rejected by you – even if done so unconsciously.

More money can mean a slew of things, so why relegate it to more problems? What about more money, better living? More money, more charity? More money, more donations? More money, more experience? Internalizing these statements as truths may not make for hit songs, but it can improve your relationship with money.

#4) Money Won't Buy Happiness

This one is hard to digest and might be more acceptably stated as "money won't solve all your problems". Either way, the concept is the same –money is not a cure-all. Again, money is a resource that can significantly improve your quality of life, but that doesn't guarantee happiness. Happiness is an emotional state that is rooted in satisfaction with your life – independent of how you view your life's quality in comparison to others.

This is why we meet people who are content with fewer material possessions, fewer accolades, more severe health conditions, and a host of other issues that could be labeled as worse circumstances. These people have discovered the truth behind happiness –that it can't be achieved in search of more. True happiness is being grateful for what you already have.

This doesn't mean we quit striving to achieve our goals. There's a difference between being appreciative of our present situation and remaining stagnant. In practical terms, we appreciate the job we have until we are promoted to our dream position. We bless the car we are driving until our new car arrives. We fill our small home with love until we can afford a bigger one.

The apostle, Paul, put it this way "I have learned to be content with whatever the circumstances" Now, that is true happiness.

#5) Money Is Not Hard to Come By

For years, poverty thinking made it extremely difficult for me to believe anything other than that "*money is hard to get & keep.*" That thought was fixed in my mind, and as a result, I lived in lack. I never seemed to have enough money to do the things I longed to do even with my high salary. Instead, I managed to only be able to get by.

This type of thinking wasn't limited to just money either. The stronghold of scarcity was prevalent in almost every area of my life. Thus, "a good job" was hard to get and keep. As was "a good man," and on and on. I never once imagined that my beliefs were partly responsible for the shortage of resources and opportunity in my life.

But when I changed my mindset from poverty to abundance, I began to manifest the very desires that seemed to elude me before. Have you ever known a person who seems to achieve everything they set out to do? What we deem "lucky" often boils down to the fact that people who believe they can, can. People who believe they cannot, cannot.

I'm not suggesting that if you tell yourself, "*I am going to make one million dollars today*," the money will magically appear. No. What I'm saying to you is this: start believing that anything is possible. You can have more money. You can have a better career. You can fall in love. You can be healed. Once you begin to think those empowering thoughts, you can more clearly see the opportunity to act.

You've heard it said, "Luck is preparation plus opportunity." We can all be lucky. We all can achieve our heart's desires, but it begins with us first believing that we can do it. When we believe we can, we are more likely to prepare ourselves and pursue opportunities. Suddenly, "I never have enough money," turns into, "I've found a neat idea that can generate additional income." What was once, "All the good men are dead or in jail," becomes, "I think I'll attend a speed dating event."

Yes, when you believe that there are enough opportunities and resources for everyone – including yourself – you experience a shift. At any time, you can choose to stop believing that you will never have enough and start believing that you can and will. And the best part is, you have absolutely nothing to lose.

If your relationship with money could use improvement, try the next exercise: write down your thoughts on money, paying close attention to whether they are positive or negative in nature. When you have completely fleshed out those thoughts, examine which of them could use adjustment. How can you bring a more positive perspective to your financial point of view? Awareness is the first step.

Exercise 4: Financial Feelings

_____

_____

_____

_____

_____

_____

_____

_____

_____

_____

_____

_____

_____

_____

_____

_____

_____

_____

_____

_____

_____

_____

Chapter 6: Others

Just as our relationship with spouses, family members, and friends can affect our thought process; our thoughts on people with whom we do not share a relationship can also impact our state of mind. Negatively labeling others whose stories we do not know and with whom we have had no personal experience prohibits us from seeing the positive in everyone. If you've lived your life thinking all homeless people are "lazy" or all convicts are "bad", you may have missed the opportunity to bless or be blessed by members of those groups.

In the same way, if you are critical of a race, creed, gender, sexual orientation, or nationality of people, those thoughts can affect not only your state of being but also everyone with whom you have influence. In today's climate, it can be extremely hard to see the good in certain people. And why try? With so many hateful and heinous acts being committed from day to day, it is understandable that many of us wish to limit our interactions with people we perceive as dangerous. But to experience a more loving world, we must start with ourselves.

And awareness is the first step. You may have every reason to dislike the bullies in your workplace, the classists at your place of worship, or the racists in your neighborhood. Your negative feelings toward these people may be justified by actions they've committed in the past. But you take away their power when you forgive them for you. When you release those angry emotions that you've held on to, your mindset will shift.

This was my experience years ago in a work environment that was extremely chaotic, stressful, and emotionally draining. The department was constantly under new management. The turnover rate was so high that employees who had been with the company for as few as three years were considered veterans. There was gossip, backstabbing, bigotry, and racism on full display daily.

And the bulk of the disparaging behavior could be attributed to a five-person group in a department of at least 50 people. This small group of tyrants took pleasure in creating a toxic atmosphere that they could control. To your face, they were chummy and polite. But behind closed doors, they were the opposite. And they were all from a similar background. It made for a horrible office culture. If you didn't belong to their tribe, you were deemed incompetent and lazy. If you dared to stand up to them, you were then labeled angry and difficult.

The years I spent in that environment reinforced a deep-rooted belief that had been planted in me some 25 years before I ever even applied to that job opening. I needed no more convincing. In my mind, everyone from this background was evil. Period. It had been my experience in life, time and time again, that this group of people were not to be trusted under any circumstance.

So, every day, I woke up and went to work in this spirit. I avoided these people at all costs. And over time, if anyone new joined the department with the same background, I avoided them too. I gave them no chance to prove the hypothesis in my head right or wrong regarding who they were. I assigned everyone in that group the labels evil and untrustworthy and carried that baggage every single day in that workplace – 809 to be exact.

809 days of anger. 809 days of rage. 809 days of unhappiness. 809 days of fear. 809 days of negativity,

and I'm not sure if even one of my co-workers had an unhappy day on my behalf. Their lives seemed to go on just fine while I stewed in disdain and discontent. Even though I had experienced discrimination at their hands, the resentment I carried toward them troubled only me.

Would I have felt better if the disregard with which I treated them negatively impacted their workplace experience? Possibly, but it would undoubtedly have been short-lived. Two things helped to bring me peace in that circumstance: changing my mindset, and what quickly followed thereafter – finding a new job!

It was as simple as recognizing the negative label I had placed upon people with a certain background, working through the cause of those emotions, and changing my mindset. Those three steps helped me rise above that environment. When I decided to let go of the anger, unhappiness, fear, and negativity associated with that workplace experience, I could see more clearly how that opportunity was no longer a fit for me. That realization prompted me to update my résumé and seek new opportunities.

Your experience may be far more complex than job discrimination. Maybe you've had deeply inflicted wounds by persons of a certain background. Or maybe you've been the one negatively assigning labels to those you do not know. Whatever your circumstances, it is never too late to rise above choosing to hate. You can always recognize your misgivings, work through the cause, and change your mindset.

Just as our bodies are fields of energy, so is the world. The vibrations we emit will return to us. Hinduism and Buddhism call it karma. Galatians call it reaping what you sow. Physics calls it Newton's Third Law of Motion. The principle goes by many names, but its truth remains the same – we get what we give. If we want love, we must give love. If we give hate, hate is what we will receive.

If we find ourselves in a situation where we cannot spread love, we can always bless the atmosphere with our absence. Changing our mindset is a choice we make for ourselves. We may have experienced trauma at the hands of certain people, but what those people do speaks to who they are. How we react speaks to who we are. We are maintaining positive vibes for ourselves because we realize that when we do, our lives elevate. When we choose to let go of our fear of others, abandon our judgment of them, and forgive them for the acts they've committed against us, we fix our thoughts on them.

Prayer #2.

Heavenly Father,

Thank You for the world in which we live. Thank You for all of Your creation and Your loving kindness and care toward that which You have created. Father, I ask that You help me to be the change that I would like to see in this world. Help me to be more loving, accepting, positive, and kind. Help me to refrain from negatively labeling those You have created – especially those with whom I have had no personal experience.

Lord, open my eyes up to biases, misgivings, and judgments I have internalized towards others. Help me to see areas in which I can improve. Help me to recognize where I have not acted in accordance with Your teachings on how to treat others. Forgive me for the times that I have fallen short in my regard for others. And give me Your Spirit in this area.

Amen.

Chapter 7: The Past

Our pasts are often filled with all sorts of memories –
positive, negative, uplifting, discouraging, enlightening,
confusing, and everything in between. It can be
wonderful to have these experiences at our recollection.
The ability to think about a joyous time in our life can
give us feelings of happiness presently. But when we
find ourselves revisiting past hurt, pain, and
disappointment, it's time to fix our thoughts.

We can indeed learn from the past, but we shouldn't live
there. We've all made mistakes that, if given the
opportunity, we would change. It could be the most
devastating incident that we've encountered in life or
the smallest misstep with severe consequences.
Whatever it is, it can't be undone. The task is learning to
live (happily) with it.

Just as our accomplishments do not define us, neither
do our mistakes. No matter how serious we perceive
our mistakes as having been, we can be forgiven. And
we can forgive ourselves. We only need to take the first
step.

A large part of fixing our thoughts includes letting go of the past. Whatever has been done, is done. We can't re-write or re-live it, and with that knowledge, we must *decide* to make the best of what is to come. Certainly, if we have wronged someone or knowingly inflicted pain upon another, we can go to them and ask for forgiveness. We may even consider putting action behind our repentance. But whether we are forgiven by others or not, *it is most important that we forgive ourselves.*

To err is human. We will get it wrong. We will make questionable decisions. We will act out of anger, ignorance, and indifference. We will not always behave in accordance with the teachings of our Higher Power or what is in the best interest of ourselves and others. At times, we may even know better and continue to choose incorrectly. However, it is never too late to begin again and change our mindset.

The voice that calls our attention to past mistakes, humiliations, failures, and disappointments is an enemy. We have the option to replace that voice with one that is forgiving, understanding, gracious, and loving. When we experience thoughts that remind us of past transgressions, we can recognize them and replace them. When the thought enters our mind, we can declare to ourselves, *"This is not helpful, so I am choosing a new thought!"*

We can take this action as frequently as necessary until it becomes a habit. To become excited about what is to come, we must let go of what has gone. Repeatedly revisiting painful experiences of the past can create a feeling of despair so deep within us that we begin to believe that there's nothing more to our lives. But when we believe that there are better days ahead, choosing to live becomes easier.

This change in our thoughts may not happen overnight. What is important is that we remain consistent and prayerful on our journey to fixing our thoughts about the past. It may help you to think about a friend or loved one. How would you react if a friend revealed a past transgression to you? Would you berate or console him? Would you call her every day to remind her of her fault? You must treat yourself with the same grace and kindness with which you would treat a loved one. Forgiveness is a process. Be patient and compassionate with yourself. And remember that you can always begin again.

On the other hand, if memories from your past always seem greater than your present-day, consider this: what is happening today will one day be the past. You will likely look back at this year, this space in life, and its memories and wish you had savored these days as well. The good news is that you can start today. You can be present in all the moments of your life and feel confident in knowing that you fully appreciated them.

What would being more present in your day-to-day life look like for you? Could it mean you spend less time working and more time with your loved ones? Is there a chance that you are detached when you are around others, mindlessly searching the internet and missing out on personal interaction? Do you need more time to restore and recharge? Are you tired and worn down from seemingly unending tasks?

Whatever your circumstances, know that you can make small changes today that can have a lasting impact on your future. You can incorporate daily prayer and meditation in your life, thus giving yourself a more positive outlook on your present-day circumstance. You can switch out TV time for time with yourself and/or the people you love. You may want to adopt a new hobby, eat healthier, get in touch with nature, or see a therapist. There are so many things you can do to prioritize yourself and make the most of your present-day moments.

Life is a journey, and at its conclusion, our story will not be about our accomplishments, titles, nor our failures. Our story will be about how we impacted others and the world. Our legacy will be the relationships we cultivated, the lives we touched, and the memories we made. To ensure that it is a good one, we must let go of the past and embrace today.

Affirmation 2:

I appreciate today and will be present for it.

I release the pain of the past and receive forgiveness for past sins.

I forgive those who have hurt me.

I am excited to begin again.

I appreciate today and will be present for it.

I release the pain of the past and receive forgiveness for past sins.

I forgive those who have hurt me.

I am excited to begin again.

I appreciate today and will be present for it.

I release the pain of the past and receive forgiveness for past sins.

I forgive those who have hurt me.

I am excited to begin again.

Chapter 8: Loss

Whether it's a loved one, relationship, or opportunity, grief has a way of bringing about negative emotions. It can be hard to accept that our lives as we know them might never be the same. The comforts we once enjoyed may be no more. What lies ahead can be both unfamiliar and unsettling.

Words may fail to console us when we experience the death of someone we hold dear. Likewise, an unwanted divorce or separation from a spouse can feel like a weight too heavy to shoulder. A layoff, bankruptcy, or judgment against us in the court of law can carry penalties that seem impossible to repay, but we can move beyond the pain of loss if we persevere.

There is no roadmap to grief. Some days may feel better than others. And at times, we may seem to regress. But if we allow ourselves to feel our emotions fully and choose to face each day as best we can, with the mindset that we will prevail, we will. Processing grief for everyone is different, but the goal is the same – to survive.

There are few things harder than living with the loss of someone we love, but it is possible if we change our perspective. That dearly departed loved one may be in a much better space – free from pain, discomfort, and turmoil. The person that walked away may have been hindering us from living the life we were created to live. The termination of our employment may force us to pursue a project that will ultimately bring us more peace and prosperity. Adjusting our perspective can help us live through the excruciating pain of loss.

It may also help us to change the narrative surrounding loss in our heads. Instead of "*Why is this happening to me?*", we can ask ourselves, "*What can I learn from this?*" If the loss of a loved one was an untimely one, leaving us with unresolved feelings or unspoken words, how can we act so that we don't experience those feelings again? If the dissolution of a relationship left us with little to no self-love or self-worth, is it possible that it may benefit us to heal those wounds before engaging in another relationship? Learning to seek a lesson in loss can help propel us into a healthier space.

We cannot fully experience life without experiencing loss. But our hearts can heal if we choose to survive.

When we allow ourselves to feel our emotions unapologetically, adjust our perspective, and seek the lesson in our loss, we can overcome grief. And we may be better for it.

Prayer #3.

Heavenly Father,

Please allow me to heal from the heartache I am experiencing. For You know the loss with which I am coping is heavy and burdensome. Lord, I ask that You break the chains of grief that bind me and allow me to overcome the negative emotions I am feeling as a result. Lord, use my pain for a purpose. Help me to draw nearer to You in my darkest hours. And help me to remain close even as I begin to see the light. Lord, I thank You for the opportunity You gave me to experience my loved one. Help me to always cherish the good times, to learn from the bad, and to move forward in peace and love.

Amen.

Chapter 9: Success

Few things compare to the feeling we get from achieving our goals. Watching our ambitions and dreams come to pass is an amazing experience, complete with a sense of victory, pleasure, and fulfillment – *at that moment.* Success feels good. Passing the course, getting the job, buying the building, selling out of inventory, and the realization of other dreams can bring us happiness and hope.

Fighting for and celebrating our wins is an essential part of our journey. It's important to know and be reminded that we can accomplish anything we set out to. Yet it is equally as important to understand that we are not defined by our successes. Working for wins is commendable, as is learning from loss. And though popular culture tells us that we must always be grinding, building, or striving for success, we must know that there is a time and place for both success and failure.

Yes, failure is just as vital as success. Not in the sense that we should aim to fail or anticipate failure, but it may help us grow and mature if we embrace failure when we experience it. How do we embrace failure? We are honest with ourselves about how we get there. We learn from the steps we took in the process. And we prepare ourselves to begin again, knowing that the experience of failure can make for sweeter success.

When pursuing our goals, it is also necessary to check in with ourselves to be sure that we're on the right track. Is this achievement for ourselves or others? Is the task we are undertaking aligned with our life's purpose or a distraction to appear accomplished to onlookers? To be successful, we must first define success *for ourselves*. Is it the accumulation of accolades and wealth, or is it the attainment of our inner peace and happiness? Whatever success looks like for us, it is easier to achieve when we are aware of what we're seeking.

Though the excitement of watching our dreams unfold can provide us with a sense of happiness, we must understand that these feelings are temporary and may diminish as time passes. When you think of the milestones you've achieved in life and how happy they made you at that moment, can you still feel those vibrations today? Even memories of the best days of our lives aren't as satisfying as they once were. And because many of us are looking to feel and be happy, the emotions associated with success are often mistaken for happiness. In the same way, the desire to be happy is often mistaken for the desire to be successful.

We can avoid this trap by recognizing that our happiness is independent of our successes. Our happiness radiates from within. It is formed from the feelings of peace and contentment that arise when we decide to appreciate both the wins and losses in life with the same grace. This becomes easier for us when we realize that *all* things are working together for our good.

Just as our victories can usher us into a greater position, so can our defeats. When we understand this concept and embrace it, we are better able to see the positive in every step of our life's journey. We can win and lose with grace; because we know that even our losses are setting us up for another win.

Losing with grace demonstrates patience and humility, and humility prepares us for success. When we have lost with grace, it is easier to not allow wins to inflate our ego. Despite how hard we feel we've worked or how huge we feel our accomplishments are, when we recognize that our worth is independent of our achievements, we are less likely to feel saddened and dejected by our shortcomings.

Freeing ourselves from the pressure of having to accomplish and needing to achieve helps us lead happier and more fulfilling lives. When we focus on defining success for ourselves – not appearing successful for others, aligning our goals with our life's purpose – not seeking accolades and wealth, and valuing ourselves independently of our achievements – not being identified by our successes, we can experience what our soul truly seeks, which is love and happiness.

If you've been driven by success and crushed by failure, try adjusting your perspective. Evaluate your feelings on success by asking yourself the questions in the next exercise. You may find that your thoughts on success need revisiting.

Exercise 5: Questioning Success?

What does success mean to me?

_____

_____

_____

_____

_____

_____

What tasks (if any) am I completing to move me closer
toward *my vision* of success?

_____

_____

_____

_____

_____

_____

What is my purpose in life?

_____

_____

_____

_____

_____

_____

What actions am I taking to walk in that purpose?

_____

_____

_____

_____

_____

_____

Who am I without my successes?

_____

_____

_____

_____

_____

_____

Chapter 10: Life

Life can be difficult. Both circumstances beyond our control and the choices that we make can cause difficulty. Poverty, heartbreak, loss, addiction, and more can hurt us so deeply that we become filled with thoughts of worthlessness, negativity, and hate. And none of us are exempt. Life happens to everyone, and it keeps happening day after day.

But God has equipped each of us with a tool to combat negative feelings – our mind. When we train our minds to see the positive in situations and to be grateful for the opportunity to rise each day, we will see a shift in our circumstances. We've been blessed with one life. We have one mind, one body, and one soul to use on our Earthly journey. Why not make the most of it?

Our story can change today if we so choose. When we become aware of the thoughts that have been holding us back from our highest good, we can change them. In the past, we may have subjected ourselves to deprecating self-talk, engaged in unhealthy relationships, or even sewn seeds of negativity, but the good news is we can leave those behaviors in the past. A sustainable change in our lives begins with fixing our thoughts.

Begin affirming to yourself today:

- My life is worth living.
- I can change my circumstance.
- I can be happy.
- It's not too late for me to switch careers.
- It's not too late for me to find love.
- God loves me.

And any other positive affirmation it takes to overcome the forces that tell you that your life is not worth living. The more you speak positivity over your life, the greater the chance you will believe it. And the moment you believe for better, better is on the way! All the forces of the Universe will conspire to usher you into a better space when you believe.

Your life has meaning. Your life has value. Your life has a purpose. You were created uniquely and equipped with everything you need to be happy. If you've suffered from depression, and the trials of life have broken your spirit, be encouraged! It can seem hard to pick yourself up from that place, but your life depends on it. Gather your strength, go to God in prayer, and begin again.

The turmoil that the enemy sent to break you will be your testimony if you turn your thoughts around. It can and will happen. You only need to take the first step. Love yourself as you would love your very best friend. Love yourself as you would love the greatest romantic partner of your life. Love yourself as God loves you – fully, unconditionally, and without reservation.

Think about the story of your life. What will your legacy be? How do you want to be remembered? Know that you can start today, embodying all the qualities that mean the most to you. You can be loving today. You can be kind today. You can be a reflection of the Creator today.

No matter what you've told yourself, nothing is too far gone for God. He can take the scraps of your life and weave them together to bring Him glory. He can use you to help bring others closer to Him. He can restore to you what was taken by the enemy. Understand that no job is too big or too small for Him. And when you cast your cares upon Him, He will renew your mind and spirit.

You may be unsure of your faith, and that is ok. You might not have a vision, direction, or plan for your life. But if you have a desire to live, that is enough to start. Today is the day you begin to make the best of your life. Today is the day that you rise to the occasion. Today is the day you become clean. Today is the day you stop contemplating suicide. Today is the day you forgive that person who hurt you. Today is the day you forgive yourself.

If you are reading this, know that God loves you. You are valuable. You are forgiven. You are redeemed. It is time for you to release doubt and step into the life you were created to live. Your time is now. Encourage yourself. Speak words of positivity over your life and walk by faith.

Know that you are not alone on this journey. When you commit to fixing your thoughts, you will receive the assistance of all the Universe. Where God leads you, He will provide. He will create opportunities for you to flourish. He will not allow you to lack.

Now the task is upon you to follow through. Rise each day with an attitude of gratitude and give your best effort. Appreciate the people in your life. Love yourself and others. Bless your current circumstance while working toward your dreams.

Abandon negative thinking and negative company. Resist the urge to sink back into your old way of being. Continue to elevate. Continue to push yourself and rise higher. Embrace the discomfort of growth. Be open to instruction.

Your new mindset is one of positivity. This new chapter in your life requires you to be bursting at the seams with love, light, and abundance. It requires you to put down your old ways. Gone are the days where you chose anger and strife. Out of your mouth now flows the overflowing of love placed in your heart.

Bless everything in your life and be the change you want to see. When you are tempted to regress, resist that temptation. And if there is a time you fall short, forgive yourself and begin again. Remember, your life depends on it.

Prayer #4.

Heavenly Father,

Thank You for placing the desire to live for You within me. Help me embrace Your Spirit every day. Help me to fix my thoughts on what is pure and lovely and to dwell on the good things in myself and others. Allow me to be gentle with myself on my journey to positive thinking and help me to get out of my way.

Lord, reveal Your purpose for my life. Help me walk in it and find happiness in Your assignment. Remove any emphasis I have placed on things that are not in accordance with what You would have for my life. Help me to begin again, keeping Your will for my life first.

I forgive those who have hurt me. And I ask that You forgive me for the transgressions I've committed. Keep me focused on building the new. Help me resist the temptation to return to my old ways. Free me from the chains of negative thinking today. Allow me to see the positive side of everything in my life.

Today, I commit to seeing myself as You see me. I commit to loving myself as You love me. I commit to showing gratitude for my circumstances and to speaking positivity over my life as You elevate me. In my darkest hours, may I remain close to You. And may You forever fix my thoughts on the things above.

Amen.